Noticing Eden

Noticing Eden

Marjory Heath Wentworth

SOUTH CAROLINA POET LAUREATE

For Pitts —
enjoy these
uncanny poems

Joy
Marjory WB

HUB
CITY

2003

ISBN 1-891885-34-0
First printing, November 2003

Cover art, *Marsh Grass*, 2000, Oil on Canvas 60"x48"
   ©Jonathan Green • Collection of Joshua & Cynthia Martin
   —Photograph by Tim Stamm
Book and cover design by Mark Olencki
Portrait, page 85, by Lauren Preller Chamber

Hub City Writers Project
Post Office Box 8421
Spartanburg, South Carolina 29305
(864) 577-9349 • fax (864) 577-0188
www.hubcity.org

Acknowledgments

Some of the poems included here have been published in magazines, newspapers, books, and anthologies. Grateful acknowledgment is made to the editors.

Appalachia: "Core Banks, North Carolina"
Brightleaf Magazine: "Hurricane Season"
Capturing The Spirit of the Carolinas: "Barrier Island"
Contents Magazine: "Carolina Umbra" and "Findhorn"
The Grasslands Review: "Irises"
Point: "ACE Basin," "Naming the Dead," The Painter's House," and "The Color of Rain"
Skirt: "The Nest of Stars" and "Wild Plums"
The Post and Courier: "Islands" (Every Day) and "Wild Plums"

"The River" appeared in *Plantation* (a novel) by Dorothea Benton Frank.
"Barrier Island" appeared in *Isle of Palms*, (a novel) by Dorothea Benton Frank.
"Contretemps" appeared in *Skyward* (a novel) by Mary Alice Monroe.
"Carolina Umbra" appeared in *The Hidden Costs of Coastal Hazards: Implications for Risk Assessment and Mitigation*, published by Island Press, 2000.
"Carolina Umbra," "Findhorn," and "The Grace that Names Them" were published in *45/96 The 96 Sampler of South Carolina Poetry* (anthology).
"Lady of the Snow" appeared in *You, Year, New Poems By Point Poets* (anthology) edited by Tom Johnson.
"Homecoming" was published in *75, Retrospective of The Poetry Society of South Carolina* (anthology).

Some of the poems also appeared in *Nightjars*, a chapbook published by Laurel Publishing (1995) and *What The Water Gives Me*, Poems by Marjory Wentworth, Art by Mary Edna Fraser published by Booksurge (2002).

I would like to thank the Virginia Center for the Creative Arts, where many of these poems were written. Grants and awards from the South Carolina Arts Commission, the Charleston Area Arts Council, the South Carolina Academy of Authors, the Poetry Society of South Carolina, and the Trident Community Foundation aided in the completion of this book.

Grateful acknowledgement is made to the Gibbes Museum of Art, the Duke University Museum of Art, and the National Science Foundation where many of the poems were exhibited.

In addition, the author wishes to extend her gratitude to William Allen, Carol Antman, Tom Blagden, Camilla Carr, Lindy Carter, Fred Chappell, Linda Ferguson, Chris Forhan, Dottie Frank, Mary Edna Fraser, Sara June Goldstein, Jonathan Green Studios, Barbara Hagerty, Howard Kaplan, Sue Monk Kidd, Kurt Lamkin, Mary Alice Monroe, Leigh Murray, Mark Olencki, Dr. Orrin Pilkey, Ellen Rachlin, Jonathan Sanchez, Governor Mark Sanford and Jenny Sanford, Denny Stiles, and Betsy Teter.

—Marjory Heath Wentworth

Table of Contents

IV.

For Peter

Love is as strong as death.
Song of Solomon

Near the Doorway

There may have been
An empty road, opening
Its hands for me.

Standing in the center of a field,
I watched fog spreading over the island
As layers of clouds streamed
Overhead. Birds in the trees
Were calling out to one another.

I couldn't tell their voices apart.
I couldn't see which branches they were calling from.

Looking down, I dreamed the earth
Was one field emptied of fog,

One house near the sea.

Dark fires burned along the shore road.

Four flames
Four directions
Salt tossed in the wind.

Rain fell at my feet.
Snow fell, far off.
Stone, star, cold, fire.

The birds suddenly silent
In the trees. I saw my voice.

I.

Barrier Island

Where nothing is certain, we awaken
to another night of delicate rain
falling as if it didn't want to
disturb anyone. On and off
foghorns groan. The lighthouse beacon
circles the island. For hours, melancholy
waves tear whatever land we're standing on.
Listen to the sea—rain dripping
through fog, suspended at the edge of earth
on a circle of sand where we are always
moving slowly toward land.

Core Banks, North Carolina

Once, whalers built their camps
atop tenuous fans of overwash,

now fishermen's junked cars
grow into drift and dune.

Infinity lives
in the damp bones of

abandoned things
buried in the sand.

There is no stillness
in the sea spilling

into prehistoric inlets
carved into the sound.

An orange arc of moon sinks
in the middle of the sky .

Now there is wind,
the resurrection of water,

starlight
drowning in the tidal delta.

Shackleford Banks

A dark dwarfed horse stumbles
beneath the diminished sun.
Caught in the salt marsh,
he crushes cattails beneath his hooves
as he runs in overlapping circles
blinded by his own noise.

Clouds rise above him,
hard and metallic, moving
until the sky is filled
like a giant jigsaw puzzle
blocking the moon
and whatever lost light
this animal could hope for.

Findhorn

The sight of the ocean
always brings me home.
My childhood was one long day
with the sea. I even believed
that souls of the dead
swam beneath the water
until it touched an edge of the sky
and became heaven.

At low tide this beach is endless,
as flat and clear as the glass
pools collecting
between the dunes and the waves.
A pale moon rises. At midnight
little white lights begin to shine
on the offshore oil rig.

They say this place is spiritual, mystical.
People in the community grow
giant cauliflower in the fertile soil.
I know nothing of the soil
and the fantastic vegetables,
but I do know
that I have never felt
closer to the dead.

I think of my father continuously
as I stare into the pink light
at the edge of the sea
where the sky is opening
to the setting sun.

Toward the Sea

The wind is an empty place. You enter
expecting something softened by the sea.
A piece of cedar shaped into a body
you once loved. Perhaps the hand that held you
from a distance or the face that simply
held you here. Still moving in and out of time
during the hour when night meets day,
you try to find your bearings.
You pick up objects. You want to remember.
Jagged edged rocks in the palm of your hand.
You hold them up in the moonlight.
They are earthbound, filling with sky.
You walk on, pause to scoop tiny iridescent
shells, the colors of cream and roses.
Little by little the air brightens into hours,
which are either empty or full of all the things
you love and remember, depending
on which direction the wind is coming from.

Windows

Where the sea holds open the palm of its hand
islands root with intelligence,
like plants in a window turning blindly
in the night to grow toward something known,
yet unknown. Fingers of water stroke the land,
that rises in rain and the unraveling
chaos of wind, running
dark-breathed and primitive. And the universe
we see reflected from these
weary hands, becomes our arbitrary home.

Our houses grow into the air's cacophony,
still we spend our lives pretending
to hear a pattern of sound woven into the wind.
From windows we have built to watch the world,
within and then without the land, we search
four corners of the metronomic sea,
from which we came composing hours
for symmetry. We hunger for the moon,
whose hand is stronger than a million
bright arms of sunlight thrown across the water

And when we feel a warm wet wind
lifting the burden of our hair,
or when love enters our lives
unexpectedly, we know how to
hold this gift in our arms. In the rain,
we watch the landscape rearrange.
Beneath our feet we feel roots reach
deep into the earth, while we remember
the simple choices we don't ever make.

Islands

Every Day

I love the way the old oak scatters sunlight
across the gray and red tin gatehouse roof.

I love the way the rain pools in ruts
between the eaves. I love the birds

that come. Each morning
I watch the purple iridescence

spread across the black-feathered
grackles gathered here to drink.

I'd like to live like them
as if light and water were all

that I required from the boundless
air surrounding me.

Memorial Day

At the bonfire on the beach, blue and pink
lights stream across the sky at sunset.

I want to fly into those veins of color spreading
over the sea. I love the night that falls upon us,

suddenly. I love the moon
pulling the sea over flames we have made.

Together, in the darkness, our hearts
are still. And we believe,

despite our many wounds, that love can be
a simple thing. Out there

beyond the blue-rimmed horizon,
anything seems possible.

My Birthday

I love surprises.
You surprise me

with a picnic in a boat,
strawberries and chocolate cake,

my favorite book
at the bottom of the beach bag.

Out at sea, we drink
champagne from the bottle,

anchor, and swim naked
in the rain. I love to watch

the rain returning to the sea,
as if it knew where it belonged.

At Capers Island it begins
to hail—a million needles

striking our skin. On our backs
beneath a blanket of waves,

we lie still in the shallow water
watching threads of lightning scatter

across the sky. I love the way
the thunder follows,

far away. The wind
blows hot then cold.

Behind us a line of pelicans
stands at the edge of the sea.

waiting for the blur of the horizon
to split again into light and water.

Hurricane Season

The blood moon thirsts. All night,
listening to unspoken prayers,
she tugs the sea beyond itself
until redundant waves retreating
wash the yellowed marshes clean.

In the heat that follows too much rain,
people crowd the churches.
On this September Sunday morning
their hymns begin to rise
and slap the winds still raging.

This is the music of bones
entwined in mortal language—

words of those who know the wind
erases every footprint carved in earth
where water, tired as a dreamer,
circling beneath oblivious clouds,
blurs the variations painted on each human face.

Into the open womb of the sea
descend the ashes of our sins.

What keeps us here? Not gravity
or light, but rust on fences, holding
every house of swollen wood, an ache
a tooth, the day moon adrift
grinding tiny islands down to bone.

Carolina Umbra

Boats fly out of the Atlantic
and moor themselves in my backyard
where tiny flowers, forgotten
by the wind, toss their astral heads
from side to side. Mouths ablaze, open,
filling with rain.

After the hurricane, you can see
the snapped-open drawbridge slide
beneath the waves on the evening news.
You go cold imagining
the enormous fingers of wind
that split a steel hinge until
its jaw opens toward heaven.

Above the twisted house,
above this island, where the torn
churches have no roofs, and houses
move themselves around the streets
as if they were made of paper,
tangled high in the oak branches,
my son's crib quilt waves its pastel flag.

But the crib rail is rusted shut.
And you can't see my children
huddled together on the one dry bed
of this home filling with birds
that nest in corners of windowless rooms
or insects breeding in the damp sand
smeared like paint over the swollen floors.

The storm will not roar in your sleep
tonight, as if the unconscious
articulations of an animal aware
of the end of its life were trapped
in the many cages of your brain.

You can't see grief darken the wind
rising over the islands. Tonight,
as the burning mountains of debris
illuminate the sky for hundreds of miles,

I see only the objects of my life
dissolving in a path of smoke.

All the lost and scattered hours
are falling completely out of time.
where endless rows of shredded trees wait
with the patience of unburied
skeletons, accumulating in the shadows.

Waiting for the Wind

Now the hurricane is turning north.
Still, the windows sealed with plywood, darken
every room in a house not made for light.
My sons, forever terrified of wind,
are lighting candles on the screen porch.
Sometimes the air is still enough for this.
Counting seconds that each flame burns,
they say the number and write it down.
They call this "hurricane science."
All day in their pajamas, they know what to do.
Their suitcases are packed and waiting,
at the front door. Hunter says, "Mom,
we've done this before, we can do it
again." All night, rolling rugs
and lifting furniture up the stairs. We gather
scrapbooks, passports, and insurance forms;
stuff the suitcases with paper. Storm updates
and weather reports fill the television screen.
The hurricane, like a giant yellow embryo,
is swirling across the Atlantic.
My husband, up for two days straight
boarding up the doors and windows,
finally sleeps in a room,
where a family of slaves once stayed
through another hurricane in another century.
The telephone never stops ringing.
By sunrise, the kitchen table is filled
with boxes of bottled water, batteries,
flashlights, peanut butter, and diapers.
We wait. Outside, yellow clouds float
across the one remaining star. I want to know
its name. I need to see it reappear
again. To know there can be light, hiding
beneath the dark walls of wind pushing
against me from all sides, like the angry waves
beating against the edges of this island.

Contretemps

The world's dark heart brought me
here, where time was hiding
in the unleashed sea.
I will stay in this fragile place
of broken trees, and birds
that teach patience as I watch them
fill the bared branches
like dark clusters of singing leaves.

I will follow the passing flock of plovers
who think faster than we see
when they suddenly turn
and flash their snowy undersides
in one bright act.

They must have heard a warning
in the lost language of the river wind.

I see the breath of God,
moving beneath still wings
of the osprey and the eagle.
Countless angels, rising from the river
with open hands and upturned palms
to hold the wings in place
as the animals glide over
this sanctuary and pull the sky
back into the universe.

II.

there are so many dead
so many sea walls that the red sun split,
and so many heads that beat against the ships,
and so many hands that have cradled kisses,
and so many things that I want to forget.

"There is no Oblivion" (Sonata),
by Pablo Neruda

Drought and Rain

The warm air sings.
My friends are dying.

Bright notes of rain
fall upon the wounded

who wander
the road of ashes

across the land.
A scattering of seeds

spreads across fields
of infinite wind. Here

time turns into nothing
more than movement

of air through bodies.
The end is silence

as we bury the names
in fields of white sunflowers.

Sorrowful
abandoned

earth, unable
to swallow this water,

the air is singing.
My friends are dying.

White death
you are

everywhere
the melody of wind.

Wild Plums

I have walked this way before. Many times,
along these tangled paths to the sea,
I have seen the cardinals flashing
from the sweet myrtle, watched lizards
raise their heads to point the arrows
of their eyes. When I move my hands
through their world of wild beach flowers,
the yellow petals bleed a little at the center
each time they burst into flower.

Today there are hundreds of small plums descending
to the earth too soon. Like you, my friends,
they are wild, ripening, and fallen
to the ground which tears their skin
until it bleeds its thick sugary juice
across the sand. Flies are flocking.
But I can only gather handfuls of fruit
or flowers that were meant to die here,
and hold them for a little while.

—*In memory of Jimmy Redman, Richard Moyes, Brian Greenberg,
and Michael Conyers.*

Heaven Ascend

—For Michael

Winter

At Christmas
when black fabric
draped your doorway,
I watched you
breathing in your bed
so quietly
that sometimes
the air dissolved
to dust inside
the cold fires
of your mouth.
Morphine
butterflies burning
on your lips,
I moved my fingers
until you felt
the rub of love.
Another friend
was singing hymns.
When you awoke
in her arms,
you were crying.
She held on to you.
She breathed
into you. Music.
Heaven ascend.

Spring

By Easter, you were
singing in church
as if you'd never left.
Your voice was
the only sound
I heard. Joy
Joy Joy.
After months of AZT
and protease inhibitors

I inhaled the alchemy
of your resurrection:
water, wine, and bread;
lilies rotting on windowsills,
palm fronds shredding
in the pews, purple
velvet on the altar.
I placed the host
on your tongue.
Heaven ascend.

Summer

Standing on King Street,
I saw you in a crowd
of friends. Through the cloud
of love, your breath was laughter—
elegant and red.
So many colors were
spinning on your shirt,
I got dizzy
watching your dreadlocks
sweep across the sky
like busy black birds.

We should all go
to the sea now,
you said,
as if a fleet
of bright convertibles
had pulled up
like magic pumpkins.

Sunlight pouring
onto your face.
Joy catching like fire.
Shoulders high
in the wind.
Heaven ascend.

Autumn

When you need me
you call me
without words

or instructions.
And I come
to you like wind
through the open window.

And I stay.
And I stay.

I am your breath,
your strength, I move
inside you like a pulse
no one else can see.

And we talk
beyond this world,
the way we always do.

In your belly
where I sit,
I watch the circle
of women
surrounding you.
Clearly they have come
for you. Infinitely
they come
from wherever you are
going without me,
going without me.

Heaven ascend.
Shoulders high
in the wind.
Your breath
is laughter
elegant and red.

Let your hair down.
Hold onto me.
Standing too still.
Shoulders high in the wind.
Water, wine, and bread
Heaven ascend.

Beach Walk

A man who looks like someone I once loved,
passes me on the beach today.
The man is with a woman. Of course, he would be
with a woman. The man I loved loves women,
not in a lascivious way. He just loves them. And he'd say it,
just like that, *I love women, you know. Always have.*
The woman is a tall redhead. She pulls a black Lab on a purple leash.
Everyone on the beach wears shorts or T-shirts and a bathing suit.
The redhead has on heels. Her shirt is black. Her pants are black.
Mysterious, now I think, symbolic. The man wears dark green sweat
pants and a gray sweatshirt. The clothes are hanging off him
in big handfuls of soft cotton. Clothes like that must feel like pajamas.
From a distance, I don't notice his missing hair or the stillness
surrounding his diminished body that seems to glide over the sand
in slow motion. His hands in quiet fists at his sides. All his energy
focused on moving his feet—one foot in front of the other foot.
His eyes look beyond the woman and the dog, toward the sea
glittering for miles in the sunlight. He is radiant
as he takes his last walk on the beach. Although exhaustion
and pain visibly press down on him like the inescapable heat,
he is completely happy to do this one thing. The only thing he's wanted
to do for months now, imagining every detail over and over again
in his hospital bed. This man who looks like someone
I once loved, looks like a man who is making love—
a man who is here, but not here.

The Mermaid

I missed you
this weekend. The weather
was glorious, and I thought
I saw you rising from the sea.

Like a mermaid with legs,
you cart-wheeled down the shoreline
the way we used to, Lisa,
when we were dancers

holding the world in our hands
as easily as we held
our beach buckets
when we were children

together. That last afternoon
from another lifetime,
those surprisingly difficult years
slipping between childhood and adulthood,

endless nights filled with wine
and conversation, concerning
love and art and politics.
Nights ending with intractable choices

we mistook for fate.
Like the embryo growing inside me.
Cancer cells were splitting
and multiplying in your bloodstream.

I heard them singing,
as they spread out
and swam through your body
in uncontrollable waves.

Hymns roared in my ears
as the subway shook
the ground beneath us
on its convoluted journey.

We spoke about the past
and the future simultaneously,

as if they were one
as if they were

the present. Death was there,
as tangible as steam.
It rose from our teacups,
dissolved into handfuls

spilling through the half light of winter.
Emaciated, bald, eroding
before my eyes; you were
already leaning toward grace.

And though we continued to speak of the ordinary,
as you stirred sugar into your tea,
it was the waterspout twirling
in your cup that caught my eye.

But when I thought I saw you
on the beach, turning toward the wall
of black rocks until the haze and sun
claimed you in a blur,

for a moment
I swear you still had hair,
spinning around your face
like a dark halo

—In memory of Lisa Cagliouso

The Nest of Stars

The night she died
stars were nesting near my window.
The wind was so still
that echoes of the sea
were the only sounds
rising from the earth
until the howl
of one human heart
filled the universe.

—In memory of Luanne Smith Havlicek

Island Time

1

Piercing the layers of night with flames
that melt the long hours before dawn,
the sun gently peels a shroud of fog
from the island. She embraces
the ripening surface of the earth,

where houses wrapped in sleep emerge from darkness
like hundreds of seeds scattered along roadsides.
Streetlights are still burning. Beneath them,
cars pass. Weary ships with passengers
given time to rearrange the memories of night,
as the day spreads itself before them
like an unwanted offering.
Each unfilled hour, ticking
ahead on the clock in their minds.

A woman rises from bed to sit
at her window and wait for daylight
to take hold of the world
spinning into place. She is
searching for a child, the ghost
of a child, a scrap, his small voice
in the wind, a carved smile
on the face of the moon—
just any familiar sign
from one of a billion stars.

And while shrimp boats glide out to sea
on the rows of first light, she watches
a dolphin caught in the marsh
swimming an endless circle
around and around itself.

2

In my house, the absolute
joy of a baby's song
pulls me from dreams. My childrens'
eyes are opening like stars,
their tiny high voices
sing the world awake.

3

But you are afraid to sleep.
To awaken means you'll feel
the womb emptying inside you,
or see the cradle
vacant beside your bed.
Suddenly you will remember
what has happened to you,
how every happy moment of your life
is buried with your stillborn son.
Each memory mixing
with clumps of dirt, shoveled
back into the earth, where time
will hold them and then
let them go. Slowly
they will return,
like small clouds filling a horizon.

4

The morning of the funeral, rain
washes dead snakes onto the sidewalks.
Outside my window, the palmetto is rocking
in the ground like a loose tooth.
It feels like the end of the world.

That night I watch
my children in their sleep,
suddenly afraid of crib death
and tree branches tapping windowpanes.
I think of my friend.
Her loss is as vast
and uncontrollable as this sea,
which we were raised on.

Sitting in a rocker at the window,
nursing my baby, I wait for the moon
to rise from the black heart of a tropical storm.
It never does. There is only an undying wind
weaving invisible ropes around the island.

Suddenly an emptied cargo ship passes
through the lighthouse beacon.
White lights along the rigging glitter

like hundreds of stars rising from the sea.
And by the time the beacon circles
again, there is nothing
but the wind singing
in the tiny high voice of a child.

—*For Jane and Butchie Rossadini*

How the Yellow Angels Hunger

There was a time when the sky
could still crack open
releasing a daily sweep of birds
and light. There was a time
before the child left the world
in a blaze of color. It was
another universe, when
a pet parrot could sit
on a windowsill all night and gaze
at crowds of clinging angels
unravel in a gauze across the sky.

If only tears were silent
feathers. If only tears could be
simply made of salt and water
or rain, creeping down the windows
of this house where death screams
from corners of every room,
forcing its breath against panes of glass
until they shatter. For the living,
there is nothing but rain-
drops hammering the rooftop
like a flock of angry birds.

Above the wounded
house where spirits gather
to chew on clouds
and weep for all of us,
there are angels.
Hidden hungry angels
with jaundiced halos
and angry fists
churning the air.

In their hands, bloom
bouquets of bloody feathers.
Little bandages of leaves
are sticking in the wind
as the building leans
its split shoulder

toward the outstretched
branches of a live oak,
which are always
reaching toward heaven.

As lamplight devours the one room
of this house, where time is
sitting in a yellow chair
that will always be empty,
the blinded bird in the window
repeats, "Goodnight moon, good-
night moon, in the great green
room, in the great green."

The world will not stop
to see this room where a smile
is spreading on the face
of the man in the moon,
stitched into halves of satin sand
dollars and stars, swimming
on a blue crib quilt
that remembers laughter—
a crush of sand in a fist of fabric.

Now the birds are mute and hidden.
Their feathers float fluorescent
like sparks on the horizon.
But the clouds will not catch fire,
though the house is glowing
like a pumpkin with too many holes carved
in its body that let in rain,
dawn, and the chaos of birds.

The Weaver

She is looking for a house where she can weep,
where memories will be locked
in the room with pink paper roses
twirling across the walls.

From the cave of her crib
for hours she watched these flowers move,
while blood dried on blankets
balled up beneath her pillow.

From windows open to her entire world,
she heard the others play until night
filled the view. She wanted to touch
branches trembling beyond the glass,

roses climbing wood, the smell of sea
and pines moving together in the rain.
Now, she tries to count the hours
of lost silence in that room—

where tiny blue eggs in a nest
were woven into a tree that touched
every cloud. It seemed beyond her.
All of life. Dreaming of days

when she could climb anything
and hold the eggs within her grip,
until the fists would tear
open with the beating

of wings, a ripple of feathers,
water, and blood. In these hands,
the blood will be her own.
Nothing wounded

will be hiding in a closet.
In this house, a beating of wings
from the bedroom. On the bed,
built in every house of unraveling nests

where we began, she will find The Weaver
in whose hands, eggshells will mend
as if this puzzle could be reassembled
in a house where she can weep.

Red Song in the Night

A woman sitting on a porch swing
holds her grandchild and waits
for water to pour
from the red air that burns
around her. Prayers of the living,
words for the dead, scatter
in a storm of blue language.
She can lose herself in the roar
of the sea, in the rain
where nothing can be mended.

The evening is hot. And summer
steam across the open faced moon
ripples like strands of hair. The child
sleeps against her breast. His mouth—
one opening to darkness,
exhaling sugar, inhaling stars.
She hears blood flowing
into petals of bitter geranium
gathered in clay pots at her feet.

Singing *Baby Boats and Silver Moon*
her voice is deep, thunder.
Soon she is lost in the bells of song.
Remembering the white gabled house,
dead deer dangling from apple trees
outside her window, the town
where mountains of wood pulp waited
at the rail station she could have run to
that night, when a handful of hours closed
in ice at the end of a dirt road.

The moon was still
not moving through her body—
too young to be torn
open in a field like a hunted animal,
too young to watch snow
melting in the streams of her brother's breath
as he moved over her.
As he pushed himself inside her,
semen and blood spilling
down her legs. Beyond his body,

beyond his hot face, the stars
continued to burn. And the earth,
frozen in layers of sleep
beneath her, continued spinning.

The Lady of the Snow

Confused by last week's thaw
birds attack the impenetrable ground
until exhaustion drags them toward the heavens,
where snow is always falling,
filling every house and every heart
with the silence of an empty church.

Up north in an alcoholic ward
my young cousin rests in a whitewashed room
beneath a crucifix. Defeated,
she is like a punished child
confined to her bedroom.

Outside the barred window
in the center of a cloister
stands The Lady of the Snow.
Sparrows tear the earth beneath her feet.
Mary, robed in white marble,
head bowed. She is gathering strength.

III.

Nightjars

On the cusp of a day, as birdsong
began braiding strands of sunlight
through night's raven hair,
I took my first breath.

Roses tore open
the wound of their mouths
releases armies of Eratos' angels.
Entering easily

they tasted of sleep. The weave
of their sentences swirled
inside me. I dreamed I was
entering heaven on their wings.

But my heart was born in silence,
though the language of ascending fire
sounded in my damp ears as if the sun
was speaking directly to me.

Exhausted by what lay ahead,
choosing emptiness, my heart began
to float cloud-like within me
as useless as a dull knife.

Love soon pierced
the sanctum, igniting
a famished wind that threads
one blind heart to another.

Hunger, which seemed to fill
my hands with choices,
was knotting my fingers together
until they were numb.

Why did joy pass unnoticed?
Her pale feathers riding
the daily circle of wind
I placed in my mouth

thoughtlessly. I swallowed
the sacred air. It tasted

stale, like a perfunctory kiss.
Only in love could I

chew on the bread of heaven,
or hold a newborn
bird in my hands and feel
the flutter of angel wings.

Though there were lovers
who scorched me
with their mouths, then left
me to unravel in the flames.

So, my heart learned
to lie still, flowering
internally on its bed
of feathers piled in clouds.

When you touch it,
like the inside of any woman,
the heart is endless and feels
soft around your fingers.

Like any woman, whose heart
and womb are woven together
by the transparent threads
of rain that trace love's path.

Angels are always there, hovering
around the edges, and roses
quietly fill the air
as I move toward you.

Whenever I find you
it is night. Your black hair
thickened by the blessing of rain,
tiny bones of rain.

And there is music—
nightjars sing as if the sun
was trapped in their throats.
The notes are rising,

filling all the empty spaces
that drift between the stars.

I can only think of you
and your heart filled with words

that touch me
like tender bandages of light
I feel them penetrate
the windows of my heart.

Distractions

Watching crows
from my window
today, I miss you.

I don't know
why these birds
remind me of you.

Spread out
over winter grass,
they fill the field

like oil flowing
in every direction.
Even the sky

seems smothered
in a dark
smoke of motion.

From bare winter
branches, they are
watching me. Now

I know
you have come
for my heart.

When the velvet
robe of wings lifts
from their bodies

in flight, feathers
flash bright blue
and you are gone.

Voice of Water

open drawbridge
starless night

steep stairs
steep to the tower

a child
in a boat

drifting beneath
a daze of darkness

eyesbluefrombeyondthesea
lapis lazuli

lost
voice rising

voice of water
voice of light

wind rushing
over waves

too many stairs
to the bridgetower

drifting boat
drifting

years
unnoticed

by the occupied
heart

too many stairs
and not enough stars

a continent
boys lost

perhaps fire
boys, boys

the bodies of boys
the tongues of men

fear of matches
fear of water

flames caught
in the sails

wind
on the stairs

finally understanding
too much blue light

perhaps fire
and the fear

will save
her

find the word
for loss

and what
is worse

Ashes

Your exquisite hands
in the winter candlelight:
smell of garlic and rain
and ancient grief.

Outside the window, an oak
opens its bare branches
beneath the cold
white flame of the moon.

Stars burning all night:
a stream of angry words, ashes
on your skin, the smell of the sky
when it begins to crumble.

The Unkempt Garden

To find love, you must
first stumble many times
through its unkempt garden,
until roses growing
wild along a fence
unfold and offer
themselves to the wind.

Tear at the flowers
with your teeth.
Let the sharp-tongued
thorns fill your mouth
with kisses. And petals,
thick as rain, will slide
their offerings into you.

Haiku Garden

Here in the garden
Where we move like amazed birds
Poems grow everywhere

Marbleized green globes
Of watermelon spinning
Against the dark earth

Satellites of seeds
And pink flesh fill our dry mouths
With sweet warm water

Herbs in the corner
Sage, oregano, and thyme
Mint flooding the air

Fingers of lime green
Cucumber poke through curled leaves
Like bashful children

Crawling up the fence
All day the moonflowers hide
Petals from the sun

Pointed pods of green
Okra stiffen their fingers
In the summer sun

Here and there, squash vines
Filling with sunlight, explode
In yellow blossoms

The Grace that Names Them

Transformed by the grace that names them
Monarch, Queen, and Viceroy;
butterflies descend, so bright
I can hear them in the garden

popping the orange and yellow
sails of their wings
against the winds cascading
onto every life. Except for these

tossed stones of sunlight
whose transcendental flights
across the horizon
make anything seem possible.

Fire is the color of the soul, and black
are the veins of its convoluted map
repeated on four wings of the butterfly
ringing like bells in the heart of a blooming flower.

Surrendering like soldiers, prepared
to die silently in the arms of their mothers
whose enormous petals fold
and flare around them,

the exhausted insects remember
silk sheets of their cocoons
as they slip toward the stem
where the scent of heaven

swirls like sleep. Across the dark
velvet sky of their bodies, bursting
with nectar, scattered
dots begin to burn like stars.

And the voice of the wind and the bells
brightly sounding out in the garden,
illuminate the sky with songs
of all the worlds' forgotten gods.

Irises

Irises bloom despite themselves,
acquiring beauty from the inherent
contradictions, like tulips turned
inside out and flaring into the bright
colors of a bruise. But sharp
green-sworded ensiform will soon outgrow
and outnumber the crumbling flowers
risen from a stem, transformed
into leaves that pierce the night
breaking like fate above
the frail heads of irises.

—*For my mother*

Bamboo

Walking beside the cane break,
she watches small bright birds
weaving through the bamboo.
They glow at the edge of darkness,
like Christmas lights strung
in the mouth of a cave.

Behind the path, water
pours from a fountain
into a pool. The sound
is delicate, like rain
or distant bells.

Bamboo is elegant
and grows deliberately,
each section joined to the next
by a symmetrical scar.
Between them, the hollow stems
are filled with light.

The stems are tough and difficult
to break like her heart, rinsed clean.
Bamboo rises from the hillsides
a cathedral of calm green.
It has taken years for her
to find this place.

In the Dream of the Sea

I call you from the open water
surrounding us, speaking
across divided lives.

I call you
from the waves
that always have direction.

Where strings of morning glory
hold the dunes in place,
I call. In winter,

when wind pours
through cracks in the walls.
Inside, I call

although my voice
has been silent
and dissolving.

In sand
pulled back
into the body

of the sea,
from the blue
house built on sand

balanced at the edge
of the world
I call you.

Drowning stars,
shipwrecks, and broken voices
move beneath the waves.

Here, at the open
center
of my ordinary heart

filling with sounds
of the resurrected,
in the dream

of the sea,
I call you
home.

Lament

If only you could touch my heart,
lie down and listen to the sad train
that passes through its center.

If only you could see
the way my heart is shifting
on the body's sands
like a moon shell
like a wooden box with black letters
like a castle
or a lost wheel
like a slashed and stranded sea turtle
tugging against the flood tide.

If only you could put your hand
into the mouth of the heart's wind
at night
into the mouth
of the loud wind
that wakes us
weeping.

If only you could help me
find the place
the wind is made.

Bring a blanket,
wine, forgiveness.

If we could gather
the bleached and broken bones
of the fish that escaped the net,
if we could scrub the bones clean
and plant them
like a garden
like a grave.

If we could only wash
away the blood
and drown the ghosts.

Noticing Eden

There is always a storm happening somewhere...
Vladimir Shatalov, Soviet astronaut

I

Back to back in bed
a woman and a man flow
away from each other.

Their thoughts dive
out into the darkness,
which wraps them

like a thick sea
holding all their
private grief.

They have forgotten
the golden rings
swirling around their fingers,

the children
drowning in sleep
down the hall.

Awake, alone, together
the man and the woman lie still
beneath an heirloom quilt

which binds them. Tonight,
their sheets feel like the worn
lining of a casket.

II

Suspended in the temporary
stillness of water, camellias
spin in clear bowls at the bedside.

There is nothing else for them to do
now. Bound only to each other,
they are rootless, drifting like a pair

of pink origami boats, with no map
or rules to guide them. In full bloom,
the flowers open to winter

III

The lovers sleep. Beyond them
there is air. Beyond the air,
emptiness. Their hearts,
no different than the planet at night,
surrounded by such palpable darkness
that sunlight is invisible.
An abandoned star
with nothing to shine on.

IV

He turns toward the world of her
body silent beside him. Spinning
in moonlight, her skin, her skin.
He inhales. He drinks.
He releases lonely hands that break
like waves across her body.

V

The man and the woman awaken
when sunlight fills their fingers
like something they could chew
or swallow. Saliva and semen—
the albumen of two lovers
noticing Eden.

In Hours Like These

I lie beside you
and listen to the wind
swirl like a river

against the window. Rain
falls. The air is still
and cold in the bedroom.

Your arm across my waist
rises and falls with each breath.
In the darkness, it looks

like part of my body.
Perhaps it is. Now
that we have lived

half our lives in this space
made by two people
we can barely remember—

two people holding
onto each other, becoming
one body braced

against the empty
years that might have
passed apart. Months

without blood
or sound, hours
emptied of laughter,

hollow childless minutes.
with no memories.
Nothing to hold on to.

Eden

Tonight I count my blessings
awake in the silence after love,
when scent is moving everywhere
in the bedroom, as if rain had fallen
during night's reconciliatory hours.

I want to stay right here
afloat in moonlight, tracing phosphorescent
rivers spilled across twisted sheets,
until I lose myself again
in mahogany rings of my love's hair.

His head of silk and blood
becomes a ball of light
within my porous hands. Amazed
to touch the wide bones of his face,
I hold everything I need.

Homecoming

If sleep has a smell, it grows here
when flowers raise their heads in the mist
to eat the light pulsing at the edge of the sky
where tapered tails of wind unwind
like roots stumbling through darkness.

After the green silence of dreams
I rise and drink the warm rain failing,
dig two holes in the ground
to plant my tired feet,
because I need to live for awhile

in the black bed of earth. On this island
rolling beneath unfurled tongues of fog,
where the scent of wet salt can turn the air
to bread in my mouth, or blanch
the dark fisted vines that never wither.

All winter, jessamine and honeysuckle
holding petals in their closed mouths,
were waiting for desire
to open them, in the wind,
to lose themselves in rain.

When he is gone my heart rearranges
within my body, where nothing seems
to move for weeks or months. Alone
I wait for his scent to return
to the empty pillow beside me.

I am like the morning glory
embedded on our fence slats,
collapsing her purple flowers
that will resurrect and inflate
with mouthfuls of air.

The smell of grass releasing
after hours of warm rain
enters the open windows of our house.
Odors move from room to room like music.
My husband listens in his sleep.

On a couch in the living room, he listens.

With children curling like kittens around his feet,
he sleeps. Beneath pages of the Sunday paper,
cradled by all that is familiar, he sleeps.
Knowing the color of love, he sleeps.

The Coming Light

The wedding procession passes through the shadows
of an old oak growing between a graveyard and a church.
All day the sun burned through its branches. Flowers shriveled
on the headstones. Little flags hung limp on black sticks.

Now it is evening, and a wind moves off the sea.
It is a wind filled with tenderness, moving
across the bride's face like his breath, in the night
when he is kissing her. Sometimes,
when she looks at him while he is looking into her,
it feels as if she is staring at the sun,
and she has to turn away. But it is too late.
She is already a woman in flames. She has forgotten
what life feels like without love. No ache and no hunger.

They have waited for twilight: to marry
in the copper-colored air that feels like water
all around and holds them up as water does.

At the doorway, she isn't thinking about the veil
slipping off her head, or whether
her grandfather's wheelchair made it over the steps.
She sees the groom waiting at the end of a tunnel of light.
At the altar, he is turned away from her. A thin crucifix
lies flat against the beige cracked stone wall.
She is certain, that before everything and everyone
there was God, filling the air
where she walks into the coming light.

IV.

The Color of Rain

Blue is the color of rain
falling in the night,
and brown is the river
that swallows rain.

Where the sun is
drowning in green
tea-tinted water,
there are colors
giving birth in the rain.

ACE Basin

Where the earth opens her mouth to the universe

Three black rivers unfurling their convoluted tongues

Ashepoo-Combahee-Edisto

Courbet's "origine du monde"

Unseen waters flowing to and from the womb

River

The river is a woman who is never idle.
Into her feathering water
fall petals and bones

of earth's shed skins.
While all around her edges
men are carving altars,

the river gathers flotsam,
branches of time, and clouds
loosening the robes of their reflections.

Her dress is decoupage—
yellow clustering leaves,
ashes, paper, tin, and dung.

Wine-dark honey for the world,
sweet blood of seeping magma
pulsing above the carbon-starred

sediment. Striped with settled skulls,
wing, and leaf spine: the river
is an open-minded graveyard.

Listen to the music
of sunlight spreading
inside her crystal cells.

Magnet, clock, cradle
for the wind, the river holds a cup
filling with miles of rain.

But when the river sleeps,
her celestial children
break the sticks of gravity,

grab fistfuls of fish-scented
amber clotted with diamonds,
ferns, and petalling clouds;

adorn bracelets of woven rain,
rise with islands of sweet grass
and stars strung to their backs

to wander over the scarred surface
of the earth, like their mothers
simply searching for the sea.

The Painter's House

The house of wind and brightly painted birds
sharpens its rooftop in the nightstream,
like a new tooth pushing
through the earth. A pulse

passes through the walls.
It could be music or the resurrection
fern taking root on the white
painted boards. Outside,

everything throbs in the dark
green. The river hums,
and the house throws open
the windows and listens.

Rooms slowly fill with alligator skulls
and wood smoke. On shelves
lined with bowls of butterflies
pearl buttons, shining chunks

of amber, books, masks
and manmade angels—
strings of owl eyelashes
feather under glass.

In a Chinese lacquered box
that should be holding
jewels, three enormous yellowed
bear teeth wait

for someone to pick them up
and think about the mouth
which held them,
with blueberries

and trout skeletons,
the tongue that tasted
water melting on mountains
so distant, we can only imagine them here

on these salted flooding plains
where swallowing such water
would alter our lives
like a conscious baptism.

The Day Moon

When the sun warms my back
like a lover's hand,
and the wafer moon suspended
over water dissolves
within me, his fingers
move like rivers, soft flames
flowing everywhere inside my body.
His tongue traces smooth paths
on my skin. His skin
swimming on my skin, aflame
in the wet light that comes
from love. The river rises.

Day To Day

Days pass without you. And hours
drifting like clouds, move through me.

You are somewhere, dreaming of rivers,
and what it takes for them to travel

to the sea. The sea is still.
The stillness surrounds me.

Cold blue bell. The world
without your voice ...

... where nothing is remembered,
except the absence

of sound. Between us,
an empty wind,

black rivers shredding
into twisted slivers of water,

mud, and sawgrass.
I listen there

for the one
clear sound

we've made—
nocturnal rain.

Naming the Dead

Androscoggin
      Mississippi
          Combahee
             Penobscot
                Edisto
                   Mohawk
                      Susquehanna
                         Ashepoo

Rivers are named to assuage our guilt
In this country
Wherever we walk
We must tiptoe over graves
Of the vanquished
Who lie beneath us
In a continuous spin of sleep
While we try to forget
The worst things we have done
But the rivers are omnipotent
They bloom and cry like newborns
We cannot live without them
Yellow bones of butterflies
Holy red maple in seed
Fingernails and feathers
Float for centuries
Until they settle
On the river bottom's
Cemetery of sediment
The cries of the dead
Rise like air bubbles
Listen to the words
Exploding in the wind
As if flails its arms
Across the surface of the water

The rivers cannot keep silent

View From St. James

Sketchbook from Nature 1791, Thomas Coram
The Gibbes Museum of Art, Charleston, SC

I

As if time were an object one could examine
under glass, we study landscape paintings
from a safe distance. Here,
two men risen in the dark dawn
bend over their work. Heads tilting
into rows of indigo, they move
like trees with forgotten roots.

Blue mist lifting from the river
swirls around their bodies. Evaporating
clouds watch everything below:
men who can't stop moving,
chimney smoke that warms a house
these men can never enter,
and rice ripening at the water's edge.

II

Two hundred years later, a paper mill
fogs the river. And rice grows
wild in the wetlands.
On St. Helena Island a woman
cultivates a little field of indigo.

All day in the museum
I teach children how to write
poems about plantations.
But I think about their parents
waiting for buses on the treeless end
of this city street—
men and women whose ancestors
taught our ancestors how
and where to plant the rice.

Rivers of Wind

For Mark Sanford,
on the Occasion of his Inauguration
as Governor of South Carolina

Today the angels are tumbling
down through heaven's door.
All along the Coosaw
they hover in a misting halo,
until the black river
shreds into the sea. Today,
as the old oak leaves spin
into bright bunches of confetti,
oysters split open their shells
and sing. At the water's edge
lilies and tickseed bloom
white and yellow candles
for the dead. All along the Coosaw
the breaths of angels
compose the air, moving in rivers
of wind across this land.

The rivers are omnipotent.
They weave through the earth
like veins, moving for thousands
of miles. There is no beginning.
There is no end, like the moss
and trillium flowing across the forest floor,
or the ravens gathered
above the sharp edges
of the Blue Ridge Escarpment.
In the gray granite cliffs,
where they build
their winter nests of twigs and fine hair
the birds caw and chortle.
Their rumble is the sound
of a wild, free place.
From these mountain tops,
it seems you can see forever—
From the sandhills to the swampland.
From the Piedmont
to the Peedee. In all directions

today, the ever-changing colors
are splashing through the sky—

because in every heart
there is a God of hope, hiding
like a tight frightened seed,
that waits for the first smudge
of sunlight to spread
across the horizon, and later
in the purpled evening, rain.

Seeds of hope are waiting
in the sacred soil beneath our feet
and in the light and in the shadows,
spinning below the hemlocks.
Hope waits in the endless
waterfalls tumbling toward earth,
transforming into rivers
that pull us through embattled centuries.
Hope waits for the waters
to still and the currents
to empty themselves of the blood
that came before.

Hope waits for a day like today.

Hope waits for this man,
who reaches across
our divided lives.

Be still.
Be silent.

There is so much light
filling the sky here.
So much conviction
in the wind now.
Watch the seeds of hope
as they scatter far,
far across this land.

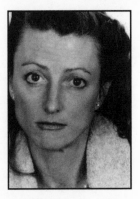

Marjory Heath Wentworth, Poet Laureate of South Carolina, was born in Lynn, Massachusetts. Educated at Mt. Holyoke College and Oxford University, she received her M.A. in English Literature and Creative Writing from New York University. Her poems have appeared in numerous books and magazines, and she has twice been nominated for the Pushcart Prize. *Nightjars*, a chapbook of her poems, was released by Laurel Publishing in 1995. Most recently, her poems have been published with Mary Edna Fraser's art in a book of poetry and monotype prints called *What the Water Gives Me*.

She teaches poetry in "Expressions of Healing"—an arts and healing program for cancer patients and their families. She also teaches creative writing at the Charleston County School of Arts. She lives on Sullivan's Island with her husband Peter and their three sons.

The Hub City Writers Project is a non-profit organization whose mission is to foster a sense of community through the literary arts. We do this by publishing books from and about our community; encouraging, mentoring, and advancing the careers of local writers; and seeking to make Spartanburg a center for the literary arts.

Our metaphor of organization purposely looks backward to the nineteenth century when Spartanburg was known as the "hub city," a place where railroads converged and departed.

At the beginning of the twenty-first century, Spartanburg has become a literary hub of South Carolina with an active and nationally celebrated core group of poets, fiction writers, and essayists. We celebrate these writers—and the ones not yet discovered—as one of our community's greatest assets. William R. Ferris, former director of the Center for the Study of Southern Cultures, says of the emerging South, "Our culture is our greatest resource. We can shape an economic base...And it won't be an investment that will disappear."